8.19.2013

Dear Mom –

A memory gift from
our visit today, we walked
amongst the work of many
and upon the shoulders of our
ancestors to arrive; to guide this
amazing piece of land – what an
opportunity!   Happy 80th year

Much love and pride to be your
daughter – Kim

COASTAL MAINE BOTANICAL GARDENS

COASTAL MAINE BOTANICAL GARDENS

A People's Garden

~

William Cullina

Dorothy E. Freeman, Ph.D.

Barbara Hill Freeman

Down East
MAINE

Photographs by

William S. Brehm - Riverside Studio: pgs 156, 166

Dave Cleaveland- Maine Imaging: p14

William Cullina: pgs 8, 12, 16–17, 23–26, 29, 31–32, 34, 36, 39–42, 44–49, 52, 55, 56 61 64–67, 71, 72, 74, 76–78, 82, 83, 86, 87–89, 92–94, 96, 99, 101, 102–103, 104, 106–112, 115–122, 126–128, 130–131, 132, 135–144, 147–149, 151, 154, 157–159, 161, 167–169, 174, 176–177, 182, 185, 191

Barbara Hill Freeman: pgs 20–21, 28, 33, 54, 58, 75, 98, 124

Daniel Haney: p100

Lynn Karlin: cover, pgs 2, 5–6, 10, 13, 50–51, 57, 59–60, 62–63, 68, 73, 80–82, 84–85, 90–91, 97, 108, 129, 150, 152–153, 162–163, 170–173, 178, 180–181, 186

Robert Mitchell: pgs 18, 59, 70, 114, 117, 125, 134, 140, 146, 159–160, 164, 184

Richard Zieg: pgs 37, 179

ISBN 978-0-89272-941-8

Designed by Miroslaw Jurek

Printed in China

5 4 3 2

Down East

Distributed to the trade by National Book Network

CONTENTS

What Is a Dream?

WHAT IS A DREAM? TO THE SLEEPER IT IS BITS OF MEMORY BLENDED AND JUMBLED with hopes and fears, then poured out on the blank canvas of the sleeping mind. To the daydreamer it is a blissful idyll that allows time to slow and the underlying beauty of things to be revealed. To eccentrics and visionaries, it is a framework for a better future that spurs them and bolsters them to keep on keeping on.

Coastal Maine Botanical Gardens has a dreamlike quality in all these senses: even the words people use to describe it speak to this: *vision, reverie, aspiration, delight, fantasy, marvel,* and *joy.* This was not a conscious intent, though it did stem from a vision of a place of beauty and connection to nature that was uniquely Maine. What I think makes this place so special is that in essence it is a group reverie—bits and pieces of people's dreams, hopes, and visions of splendor poured out onto the canvas of this exquisite little piece of rock and spruce perched on the edge of the continent. It is a distillation of what is positive about humanity—joy and hope, love and ecstasy—in a natural setting amplified just slightly so its underlying beauty is more easily seen.

When dreaming we are childlike, open and willing to explore those places that our waking mind bars us from. At its best, I think this garden has a similar effect on visitors. Maybe it is the unexpectedness, complexity, or the sheer brilliance of color, but it is very common to see guests arrive with that harried, bored, or slightly grouchy look so common in our busy world, only to see them leave hours later with a smile on their face and a youthful lightness in their soul. In a time when we are exposed instantly to all the troubles of the world through radio, television, and the World Wide Web, places like this are an indispensable antidote to noise and despair.

I for one am thankful every day that I can be involved with something that celebrates life, splendor, and joy. Call me a dreamer, but I believe the world would be better off if we all spent a little more time in the garden.

—*Bill Cullina*
Executive Director

An Unexpected Garden

"I have great faith in a seed.
Convince me that you have a seed and
I am prepared to expect wonders."

— Henry David Thoreau

FIRST-TIME VISITORS TO COASTAL MAINE BOTANICAL GARDENS ARE NEVER QUITE PREPARED for what they encounter here.

Perhaps it's the discovery of a world-class botanical garden located not in some large, crowded urban area but on a small peninsula with a population of only a few thousand in rural midcoast Maine. Maybe it's just the concept of a "botanical garden" that catches them unexpectedly: a place of beauty certainly, but also a place of ideas, education, and research.

Of course the sheer spectacle of the place is a surprise. The explosion of color, diverse flora, majestic trees, bold granite outcroppings, tidal shorefront, and intriguing sculptures is simply not what you expect to find tucked into the woods of Maine.

The more garden-savvy visitors are amazed to see the range of plant life flourishing here—exotic-looking grasses, delicately blossomed roses, curiously shaped trees. Fail-safe warm-weather annuals like marigolds and petunias are not in evidence, and scores of unusual plants burgeon here. Clearly this cannot be the horticulturally challenged Maine that is reputed to have only two seasons: the Fourth of July and winter. In these gardens nothing seems to be struggling. Everything is lush.

And once visitors begin to hear the story of how the Gardens came to be, the whole enterprise seems all the more unbelievable. Unlike the majority of botanical gardens that arise from a wealthy benefactor's estate or as an offshoot of a larger institution, this one is a decidedly grassroots effort. Dreamed up and developed by a group of local civic leaders and garden lovers more than twenty years ago, it still relies exclusively on volunteer help and the beneficence of donors, with only a small professional staff to oversee it all. It has been incorporated as an independent, nonprofit charitable organization right from the beginning. It is "owned" only by the people who enjoy it. In a very real sense it is a people's garden.

More than anything else, it is the uniqueness of the Gardens' planning and vision that is so unexpected. The philosophy of Coastal Maine Botanical Gardens has always been based first and foremost on staying true to its Maine roots: understanding what the land here uniquely wants to be and incorporating that into the design; appreciating the biodiversity of the coastal habitat; and celebrating the indigenous plants as well as those that also can thrive here.

"It is not a cookie-cutter garden but one that speaks to Maine by virtue of the design, hardscape, and plants," declares Dr. Michael Dirr, renowned horticultural author, speaker, and researcher. "I have visited many gardens; this one has a soul."

In fact, it does have a soul, and that soul is Maine. Without the Maine setting, the Maine climate, and the Maine people, this extraordinary garden would not exist. And the story behind Coastal Maine Botanical Gardens is as unexpected in many ways as the gardens themselves.

LEFT Large stepping stones in the Bibby and Harold Alfond Children's Garden pond allow youngsters to get "up close and personal" with some of Maine's aquatic wildlife. Tadpoles and minnows are so accustomed to visitors now that they float just out of reach.
OPPOSITE Cool summers allow towering blue delphiniums to thrive here as they do in few other places in the eastern U.S.

Dreamers and Doers

*"Never underestimate the power
of a small group of people
to change the world."*

—Margaret Mead

HOW IS IT THAT A CASUAL CONVERSATION BETWEEN TWO FRIENDS IN BOOTHBAY, MAINE, back in 1991 could have garden lovers across all New England and beyond talking about the "Miracle in Maine" twenty years later?

"I remember it clear as day!" exclaims Rollie Hale, a longtime Boothbay Harbor storekeeper. "I was planting 'Mr. Lincoln' tea roses and talking to my friend Chip Griffin. We were talking about display gardens at the time, and he said, 'You ought to start a botanical garden.' When things like this happen, you don't know where it's going to go so you don't record it. But I know it was in the spring of 1991."

Within weeks, Hale and a small band of like-minded dreamers gathered on the back porch of Alice West's home on Southport Island to explore the "crazy idea" of a botanical garden. Each was a lifelong Mainer or a longtime transplant to Maine's midcoast region and all shared a love of gardens, but other than that they were from a variety of different backgrounds and ranged in age from their thirties up into their eighties. Alice West was a worldwide traveler who visited gardens wherever she went. She had a passion for plants, an abiding optimism, and a quiet, nurturing demeanor. Mullie Soule, from nearby Wiscasset, brought a great knowledge of meadows and wildflowers to the discussion. Rollie Hale, a self-taught gardener, viewed the project from the perspective of a small-business owner: such gardens could provide economic development opportunities for local families.

OPPOSITE The site of Coastal Maine Botanical Gardens was a spectacular piece of Maine even before it was chanced upon by the founders. Except for the central gardens and miles of trails today, the 248 acres are still almost as densely wooded as when the early Wabanakis walked here.

Maggie Rogers, a former president of the Garden Club of Wiscasset, loved birds and flowers. As an adventurous traveler and participant in Elderhostel programs, she had visited gardens around the world and was excited by the educational potential of a botanical garden. Local nurseryman Bob Boyd, owner of Boothbay Region Greenhouses, brought professional experience and a native Mainer's point of view to the enterprise. Claire Hunt, president of the Boothbay Region Garden Club and a former elementary school principal who had retired to Boothbay from Michigan, had the leadership experience and speaking skills to carry the story to essential civic groups that could help the idea become a reality. And Ernie Egan, a lifelong summer resident of Boothbay, was a retired nurseryman from Connecticut and an ardent rhododendron hybridizer. Although each of these people brought differing perspectives and life experiences to the meeting, all were tantalized by the idea of a *botanical* garden. "That was never a point of contention," recalls Bob Boyd. "It was always meant to be a botanical garden."

ABOVE Visitors to the Gardens today, with its lushly blooming plants and hardscape that looks like it's been in place for years, have a hard time imagining all that went into creating it. This unusual panorama of the Alfond Children's Garden under construction in 2010 captures the magnitude of the job.

BOTANICAL GARDENS EVOLVED FROM THE ORIGINAL GRAND PLEASURE GARDENS OF antiquity, grown primarily for their ornamental beauty, and from the monastic gardens of the eighth century, in which medicinal herbs were cultivated as well as other flora. For much of the nineteenth and early twentieth centuries they served as living museums of plant collections. Ultimately they incorporated conservation and sustainability of plant species into their mission, which today includes horticultural education and research as well as artful display gardens. While there were some 200 botanical gardens and arboreta in North America in 1991, Maine—despite its worldwide reputation for natural beauty—was one of only three states lacking one. To those gathered on Alice West's back porch, this was an affront.

Quite quickly the group learned they had many more questions than answers. Was the notion of a botanical garden in Maine actually feasible? What should it look like here? What should it include that would make it distinctive? Where could it be built? How much would it cost to create and maintain? Where would the money

And third, research would be a key component of the Gardens. Native plants would be a priority for study, starting with the healthy stands of indigenous orchids and ferns on the property. Trial gardens would fulfill part of the research mission.

Priority number one, the board of directors realized, was finding the right land in the right place at the right price. Without a piece of land, the Gardens remained only an abstraction, which would make fundraising problematic. From the beginning, though, the founders were not looking for a site that was simply accessible or affordable; they realized that their lofty aspirations demanded a site that was extraordinary. The quest for the perfect property took two years and ranged up and down the midcoast from South Freeport, just north of Portland, to Camden, some seventy-five miles farther east.

A HIGH POINT IN THE SEARCH CAME WHEN THEY LOCATED A SEEMINGLY SUITABLE forty-acre site along Route 27 in Boothbay. It had some interesting natural features and was right on the major highway to town, but still there were doubts about it. To address these reservations, former board member Cathy Conn, who had completed several landscape design courses at Radcliffe College down in Cambridge, Massachusetts, suggested that they ask her professor there, Todd Richardson, whether he might consider involving his graduate students in doing a feasibility study of the property. Richardson, she knew, in addition to being a faculty member in landscape design, was also a resident of Maine. Very readily he recognized the benefits for his students and for the Gardens in taking on a class project of this nature.

In early 1994, he brought fourteen young men and women up to Boothbay for an intensive three-day investigation of the forty-acre property to assess whether it had all the components that the board needed for their prospective botanical garden. The budding landscape architects listened carefully to the wish list that included garden spaces, natural landscapes, water features, trails, learning activities, and visitor experiences, then set out on the acreage under consideration to determine how well the site and soils could accommodate everything.

Their findings were an eye-opener: forty acres, they reported, would be entirely inadequate for the multifaceted botanical garden that the board envisioned. In order to have space for all the features the board wanted, the Gardens would need a minimum of 100 acres of mixed topography—and it should include a stretch of shore frontage. It was a setback of sorts for the board, as the report erased another possible property from their list, but it was also a valuable lesson. By proceeding slowly and investing in professional expertise, they had saved themselves from what would have been a crippling error. Also, the findings and drawings the Radcliffe students produced explained the acreage requirements and specific soil-quality needs in such detail that they would prove valuable for years to come.

OPPOSITE Enigmatic and startlingly beautiful, pink lady's-slipper orchids (*Cypripedium acaule*) thrive in the woodlands of Coastal Maine Botanical Gardens. A long-term population study of these indigenous orchids begun in 1998 enlists volunteers to survey and catalog all the plants in three research areas during their peak bloom in late May and early June.

concept but didn't necessarily want a botanical garden in their own backyards; state botanical societies that had a few members who looked with disdain upon the Boothbay upstarts; and other local nonprofits in the region, who were concerned that there were only so many charitable dollars to go around.

Hunt became the voice of the Gardens and addressed all these attitudes head on, speaking to scores of garden clubs and church groups, appearing at grange halls, Elks clubs, Rotary breakfasts, chamber of commerce gatherings, and master gardeners meetings. "Ultimately I got so involved I ran for president of the Garden Club Federation of Maine and was elected," she says. "That gave us entrée to about fifty garden clubs throughout the state, and they had nearly 3,000 members. Since we had a free presentation, we were really, really popular because none of the clubs had to pay us for the program. I spoke in every church basement you could imagine."

Despite the early skepticism, though, the response to the first public fund-raising campaign was gratifying. In less than eight weeks, the charter membership campaign secured an astounding 180 members. The number surged to 551 in the space of a year, and these new members included not only local residents, but also people from communities throughout Maine and even out-of-staters "from away." The actual demographics of the supporters were just as heartening. "People from all walks of life became charter members," according to Boyd. "We deemed that group of 551 our feasibility study of how people would respond to a botanical garden that had no gardens." With each membership costing from $100 to $1,000, the young organization at last had some operating capital.

And during the next year, they began to use their money—ever so judiciously. Before moving forward on building the Gardens, the newly purchased land was carefully studied. Botanists and trained volunteers inventoried the existing flora and fauna. Wetlands were identified and mapped. Special features of the site were recorded on topographical maps. Native plant collections were established. Hundreds of photographs were made documenting what was already there. Horticultural experts were enlisted to teach classes and offer workshops. And research projects on populations of mushrooms, native ferns, and lady's slippers were undertaken with discipline and scientific rigor.

HOW WAS THIS ALL ACCOMPLISHED? AT THE TIME THE PROPERTY WAS PURCHASED, COASTAL Maine Botanical Gardens still had no paid staff. No way could it afford to meet even a small payroll. But what the fledgling organization did have was a growing number of volunteers, many of whom had professional expertise they were willing to donate. Recognizing this enormous asset, the directors back in 1993 had created a "board of advisors"—a corps of about thirty volunteers that included master garden designers, horticulturists, botanists, attorneys, administrators, and foundation

OPPOSITE Brilliantly colored candelabra primroses (*Primula* x *bullesiana*) and water iris (*Iris laevigata* 'Variegata') bloom in the Lerner Garden of the Five Senses. Though not completed until 2009, this sensory garden was one of many innovative ideas that came out of a charrette put together by the board in 1998 to draft a master plan for the Gardens.

directors. Included in the mix, for instance, were the past president of the New England Wild Flower Society and the former president of the American Association of Botanical Gardens and Arboreta. Empaneling this board of advisors—which in 2002 became the board of overseers—would become one of the most important early decisions of the Gardens' board.

In addition to the intensive study of the property, miles of trails were also cut in 1996 and 1997—all by volunteers using their own tools. "Wheelbarrows, pickaxes, shovels—that was it," recalls charter member Larry Townley. "We had nothing, no motorized equipment. It was all done by hand. We would push those wheelbarrows up and down the hills and hack away at the rocks and try to make something reasonably accessible." Tellingly, those early trails built with the sweat equity of volunteer labor were so well located that they remain the basis of the trail system in the Gardens to this day.

By 1998, the organization had grown to include 900 members and 129 volunteers, and there were scores of ideas among these people about what Coastal Maine Botanical Gardens should ultimately look like. A public meeting early that summer generated dozens of suggestions of what the Gardens should include, and the organization was finally strong enough financially to begin work on a formal master plan. Was it all that important to have a plan at this still early stage? "Absolutely," insists Boyd. "We always knew that we should have a master plan to go by! The only question was when we could afford to do it." Having refinanced the original three-year bank note to a ten-year mortgage, the board at last had the resources to concentrate on expanding programs and advancing the planning process that would serve as the blueprint for the Gardens for the next fifteen years. To accomplish this, the board voted to hold a charrette, a classic collaborative decision-making gathering, involving a variety of outside experts.

Coordinated under board member Bob Boyd's direction, this charrette took place over three days in late August 1998 at the local YMCA's Camp Knickerbocker on Barters Island Road in Boothbay, directly across from the Gardens' site. The thirty participants included landscape architects, conventional architects, horticulturists, student observers, technicians, a surveyor, a civil engineer, a soil scientist, and a wetlands specialist as well as board members Claire Hunt (vice president), Bob Boyd (chair of the planning and steering committee), Foster Stroup (co-chair of buildings and grounds), and Merlin Smith (member of the planning and steering committee). Group members were divided into three teams, each led by a landscape architect, and asked to sort out all the possibilities and constraints of the whole 128-acre site of the Gardens and its distinctive features.

By the final day of the charrette, the three individual team conclusions were melded into a single four-part conceptual plan that the entire group felt would meet the Gardens' unique promise of becoming a twenty-first-century botanical garden. The first component of the plan addressed natural areas, stipulating that 40 percent of the site should remain natural, interrupted only with access trails, overlooks, and meditation areas for the public, so as to protect the natural habitat that included half of the plant families known to exist in Maine. The second dealt with what were termed enhanced natural areas, stipulating that in these parts of the Gardens only plant materials related to existing flora (i.e., ferns, mosses, and wildflowers) would be added to extend the natural collections.

BELOW Yes, heavy equipment—including a crane—was used to create the Gardens. It was a memorable day when this five-ton leviathan was lowered into place on the entrance terrace of the Alfond Children's Garden. The large boulder was found on-site and carved by sculptor Carole Hanson.

The third component of the plan addressed the cultivated gardens, specifying that there be permanent gardens showcasing specific styles and types including perennial gardens, shade gardens, shrubs and broadleaf collections as well as landscaping ideas. The fourth component, focusing on the campus area, suggested it include demonstration gardens for youngsters, seasonal displays, and universal accessibility. Additionally, the campus would need buildings to house a visitor reception area, artistic displays, a library, and office space, and in the future a conservatory for year-round plant study and public enjoyment.

These components of the conceptual plan emanating from the charrette formed the foundation of the next two steps, the design plan and the construction plan, which were completed over the next several years by some of the top landscape architects and contractors in the nation and in Maine.

IN 2001 THE BOARD TOOK A MAJOR STEP BY HIRING THE GARDENS' FIRST EXECUTIVE director. New Hampshire native Tom Flood came to Boothbay after serving as superintendent of landscape services at the University of Missouri and director of the University of Missouri Botanical Garden. His two-year tenure was marked by considerable growth: the board of directors expanded in size to eighteen, the corps of volunteers grew to more than 200 women and men, and the research library was enlarged under the expert care of volunteer librarian Pat Jeremiah.

Aggregate revenues in 2002 (including $100,000 in grants and donations) grew to $685,000—a doubling of revenues over 2001. Since 1995, the Gardens had relied on donations from annual appeals for operational support, as well as income from special events and membership dues augmented by a succession of modest but morale-boosting gifts from foundations and trusts to cover mortgage payments, underwrite exhibits, and expand educational programs.

Maureen Heffernan came on board as the second executive director of the Gardens in 2004, bringing a wealth of experience in educational and special events from her nine years as director of public programs at the prestigious Cleveland Botanical Garden. She was widely known and respected among horticultural institutions across the nation and was particularly skilled at building effective professional staffs.

The next eight years under her guidance was a period of nonstop activity that included overseeing the design and construction of more than a dozen gardens, developing roadways, broadening the scope of art exhibits, educational offerings, and cultural events, expanding the staff to twenty, and fundraising that was virtually peerless in Maine. Perhaps Heffernan's most noteworthy contributions were to encourage the board to keep assessing and refining its goals and to attract world-class talents to Boothbay, Maine. It was she who asked Herb Schaal, a widely acclaimed landscape architect from Colorado with whom she had successfully collaborated on a previous project, to complete the final landscape master plan for the central gardens.

SCHAAL'S COMMITMENT TO DISCERNING WHAT THE LAND "WANTED TO BE" WAS PIVOTAL to the team of design, planning, and construction professionals who shaped the Gardens. When asked to characterize his philosophy, he compared his guiding principles to those of Frederick Law Olmsted, the renowned architect of New York's Central Park: "I am interested in creating a timeless place, having an eye

OPPOSITE Granite steps at the Vayo Meditation Garden seem as ageless and permanent as the mosses and bunchberries that flourish beside them. Most of the hardscape at the Gardens was designed to harmonize unobtrusively with the Maine woods.

Lerner Garden of the Five Senses, which would open two years later.

In 2008, more than 48,000 visitors came to the Gardens and memberships rose to 3,000. The Harold Alfond Foundation, established by the well-known Maine philanthropist, offered a $1,500,000 matching grant, which was met within eighteen months. "You know what falling in love feels like? That's what it was to us," recalls his daughter-in-law Barbara Alfond. Harold had such a good time when we initially visited the Gardens. He wasn't a botanist, but he was a huge booster of things of beauty and children. He took a shine to the Gardens right away. I think we knew it would be a hit: such a sense of playfulness, such a sense of place, something electrifying about it all."

ALSO IN 2008 A STRIKING NEW STONE WATERFALL WAS INSTALLED IN THE Giles Rhododendron and Perennial Garden, and the Burpee Kitchen Garden was planted based on a design by University of Maine horticultural design students.

While progress on garden construction continued apace under Heffernan's direction, the educational programs of the Gardens also expanded dramatically. Courses on all facets of horticulture, from designing ornamental gardens to cultivating herbs and raising vegetables in Maine, were developed for the public, as well as a full calendar of special events ranging from the Maine Fairy House Festival in August to the Frozen Turkey Hunt in November and Christmas Market in December. Also scheduled each year were dozens of garden rentals for weddings, receptions, business meetings, and children's birthday parties.

When the Lerner Garden of the Five Senses opened in 2009 it was heralded as "cutting edge" by the *Portland Press Herald* for its focus on accommodating people with disabilities. "As the name suggests," it said, "the one-acre garden is all about touching, smelling, tasting, hearing, and seeing." It cited one of the garden's early members, Mollie Moore, for helping provide the impetus for such a garden after losing her own sight a few years earlier due to a bout of meningitis. "I've been to a lot of sensory gardens, and most are fragrant and have a water fountain for a frame of reference for blind people, but they're not involving all five senses as this one is," she explained. "The whole point of this was to make a garden that can be enjoyed and accessed by everyone. I think one goal was to show people with disabilities not to give up, you still can do a lot of things." Executive director Maureen Heffernan estimated the cost of this garden at more than $1 million. "A public garden is usually a place to look at," commented benefactor Dan Lerner, "but in this one you can experience it with all five senses. What a great thing to be able to do." That year attendance at the Gardens rose to 56,350.

The next year, Coastal Maine Botanical Gardens' need for a state-of-the-art education center, a place for meetings, classes, and presentations, came to the

OPPOSITE It isn't just the profusion of bloom that is dazzling at the Gardens. Sometimes a solitary blossom can be the highlight of a visit. Here a hardy water lily opens, spreading its heady fragrance in the Lerner Garden of the Five Senses.

LEFT This magnificently understated waterfall in the Giles Rhododendron Garden was commissioned by friends of John and Sarah Giles to honor them for their outstanding leadership over the years.

attention of the family of Dr. Ed Bosarge, mathematician and longtime champion of green energy. To fund a model structure that could qualify for Leadership in Energy and Environmental Design (LEED) platinum status from the U.S. Green Building Council, they pledged a gift valued at $2 million accompanied by a $1.5 million challenge. The 8,000-square-foot Bosarge Family Education Center opened in 2011. "There's an obvious passion [my wife] Marie and I feel for the beauty of the Gardens which combines perfectly with the precision of environmental science I appreciate as a scientist," explains Dr. Bosarge.

Also in 2010 the Bibby and Harold Alfond Children's Garden opened, which very quickly became one of the most popular and most talked-about parts of the Gardens. This fanciful two-acre garden has innumerable features to delight kids of all ages—flowers and plants in every size, a treehouse, topiaries, a story barn, and even live chickens. Some would argue it was too successful. "I was going down to do my readings stint in the Children's Garden," reports volunteer Pat Jeremiah, "and I walked past a father carrying a screaming, struggling little boy. I mean, this kid was just in a rage, thrashing around and shouting, 'I don't want to go home! I want to live here!'"

Like the Lerner Garden of the Five Senses, the inventiveness of the Children's Garden captivated visitors of all ages. "Botanical gardens that we have been to previously—Kew and the Cornwall Eden Project—they're all totally different," explains charter member Helen Norton, "but there's nothing like the Children's Garden, there's nothing like the Garden of the Five Senses. At other gardens, it's more just a lot of plantings and an almost parklike setting. It was exciting to see the Garden of the Five Senses open and the Children's Garden, but it was just the progression and the thought that went into it."

Board member Ina Heafitz and her husband Lew endowed a lecture series of nationally known experts in horticulture, the arts, and sciences that launched in 2011. "Beyond the delightful sights, sounds, and smells of the Gardens," board president Susan Russell points out, "the learning and educational experiences are part of watching the Gardens grow and, in the final analysis, may be the most enduring." Visitors in 2011 exceeded 87,000.

Also that year the Gardens' first plant and garden curator, Bill Cullina, was asked to become the new executive director after Maureen Heffernan left to become executive director at Myriad Botanical Gardens in Oklahoma City, Oklahoma. Cited by his predecessor as "well-known and esteemed at the very highest level of American horticulturists, plantsmen, and garden writers," before coming to the Gardens in 2008 Cullina had developed the largest native-plant nursery in New England during his thirteen years as nursery director at the New England Wild Flower Society in Massachusetts. He is also author of five important reference books on plants and a popular lecturer and teacher for garden, conservation, and professional horticultural groups across the U. S. and Canada.

WITH TIME AND A SERIES OF SUCCESSES, THE EARLY RESISTANCE TO THE GARDENS HAD not only receded by 2012, but shifted to widespread support throughout Maine.

As a board member, volunteer, and benefactor, Ginger Carr says she has been struck by the nearly universal change of heart: "To the community, the Gardens were initially pie-in-the sky—not many people believed it would ever happen. And I can remember there was definitely resistance and a bit of jealousy," she adds. "But at a dinner party a couple of years ago, a man apologized to my husband for remarks he'd made in the past. He said the Gardens had really come to be a wonderful thing and great for the economy."

Indeed, an independent analysis by Professor Todd Gabe, of the Department of Economics at the University of Maine, recently reported the Gardens' regional economic contribution totaled $11.3 million in 2010. That included overnight-visitor spending, employment income, and capital investments. The intangible economic effects of the Gardens on the image of Maine and the midcoast area are harder to calculate, but likely substantial as well.

While the overall economic impact of the Gardens twenty

BELOW Unsung heroes of the Gardens are the many contractors, builders, craftspeople, and artists—mostly from Maine—whose fine work is on display here. No one would believe the pains taken by the stonemasons from Jorgensen Landscaping, of Bath, Maine, in testing the water flow over the Giles waterfall during its construction.

years after its founding is significant, however, the organization still relies enormously on its individual supporters. From fewer than 600 charter members in 1996 to the more than 8,000 members and donors who annually give upwards of a half million dollars to support day-to-day operations in 2012, the consistency and generosity of small and mid-size gifts from friends remain the backbone of philanthropy at the Gardens.

This broad-based support is not as visible as the dazzling gardens, but it is actually one of the most impressive parts of Coastal Maine Botanical Gardens and intrinsic to its character. From the start, it has been a volunteer-driven organization. The first paid staff did not appear for nearly a decade. It was volunteers who conceived the idea of a botanical garden, established it as a charitable nonprofit, searched for a site, secured the loan, hand-cleared the land, marketed charter memberships, appealed for donations, wrote grants, published newsletters, conceived ideas for specialty gardens, counted lady's-slipper orchids, held fundraisers, taught workshops, marveled at a succession of guardian angels who appeared on the scene to help out, and kept believing in the promise of the Gardens through it all.

THE WORK OF TODAY'S VOLUNTEERS MAY HAVE CHANGED A BIT, BUT NOT THEIR ZEAL, JOY, and professionalism. After twenty years, the Gardens is blessed with indispensable, well-trained, and committed men and women who volunteer as garden docents, Children's Garden stewards, Visitor Center ambassadors, gift shop clerks, shuttle drivers, surveyors, membership assistants, interns, caterers, grounds workers, poster distributors, salespersons, ticket-takers, storytellers, workshop assistants, and greeters. Six hundred determined volunteers donate more than 10,000 hours annually to the Gardens today. Without volunteers, the Gardens simply could not exist as the world-class botanical garden it has become.

"Observing the transformation of this land into New England's largest botanical garden has been thrilling!" offers benefactor Karen Bartholomew. "I'm so proud of the founders for their vision and perseverance. I was blessed to know most of them. Every time I walk past the Founders Grove, I think about them and all the remarkable progress we've made since they first sat on Alice West's back porch."

But their dream continues. Dreamers and doers in their ever-growing numbers are still striving to secure a strong future for Coastal Maine Botanical Gardens. The story is just beginning.

OPPOSITE Looking over the colorful Rainbow Terraces in the Alfond Children's Garden, it is hard to believe that only a few years earlier nothing in this image existed. That is a true testament to the vision, leadership, and dedication of all the individuals who have worked to make this "people's garden" what it is today.

Visitor Center
&
Entry Walk

C OASTAL MAINE BOTANICAL GARDENS' VISITOR CENTER AND THE GARDENS AROUND IT were completed in 2006. Designed by Quinn Evans Architects of Washington, D. C., the 9,500-square-foot gateway facility houses the reception area, Gardens Gift Shop, and Kitchen Garden Café, as well as staff offices, a resource room, and library. This Shingle-style building was designed to accommodate 75,000 annual visitors—the number that planners felt was the most the Gardens could ever hope to see. When this number was exceeded in the third year of operations, it became obvious that extensive modifications to the building would already be necessary. The opening of the Bosarge Family Education Center nearby allowed half the staff to move to new offices, freeing up larger quarters for the gift shop and kitchen. The current space allows kitchen staff to serve distinctive, quality fare with a local flair to more than 30,000 guests annually. Further renovations to the former gift shop space in 2012 allowed expansion of the admissions desk, creation of a new membership office, and a library and resource room where visitors can have questions answered and access our FloraFind plant database and mapping tool. This innovative program lets anyone search for particular plants, photographs, or garden elements and to create customized tours for themselves over the Internet.

The Entry Walk gardens leading to and from the Visitor Center provide a transition between the native conifer forests that ring the entrance drive and parking areas and the colorful ornamental gardens just beyond the center. These welcoming gardens are a mix of native trees, shrubs, and ground covers blended with garden stalwarts such as daylilies and hostas along with unusual exotics, including clumping bamboo and Japanese Jack-in-the-pulpit. This marriage of the wild and the cultivated is repeated throughout the gardens to convey a sense of local context while providing novelty and horticultural interest.

OPPOSITE Guests enter Maine Coast Botanical Gardens on this stone-dust path leading up to the Visitor Center from the parking areas in the woods beyond.

ABOVE This simple mix of wild hay-scented ferns (*Dennstaedtia punctilobula*) and an exotic redbud hazel shrub (*Disanthus cercidifolius*) from Japan typifies the artful blending of native and ornamental plants along the Entry Walk. **OPPOSITE** Inside the Visitor Center a vaulted ceiling and handsome architectural detailing greet guests entering Kerr Hall. This commodious space in the middle of the Shingle-style building serves as a gathering place, event venue, and art gallery.

Four-foot plumes of goatsbeard (*Aruncus dioicus*) turn heads on the Entry Walk in June and July. OPPOSITE Nearby lilies such as this Lilium 'Brasilia' hint at the floral spectacle to come.

Autumnal hues sweep along the Entry Walk in October. In the foreground, redbud hazels smolder while orange sugar maples (*Acer saccharum*) and yellow summersweet (*Clethra alnifolia*) add to the fiery composition.

Bibby and Harold Alfond Children's Garden

T

THANKS TO A VERY GENEROUS CHALLENGE GIFT FROM THE HAROLD ALFOND FOUNDATION, the philanthropic legacy of the Maine founder of the Dexter Shoe Company, the Bibby and Harold Alfond Children's Garden officially opened to a crowd of more than 3,000 people on July 8, 2010. The most ambitious garden to date, it encompasses two acres of woods, ponds, and intensively designed theme gardens inspired by well-known children's books by Maine authors. Here you'll find spouting whales from *Down to the Sea with Mr. Magee,* by Chris Van Dusen; the colorful skiff *Tidely-Idley* from *Bert Dow, Deep-Water Man* and the bear cub from *Blueberries for Sal,* both by Robert McCloskey, a barn and vegetable garden from the E. B. White classic *Charlotte's Web;* rocks that resemble dragons from *The Stone Wall Dragon* by Rochelle Draper; and the list goes on.

The aim here was to create a garden that celebrates wonder, discovery, and fun; a garden for kids of all ages that would still be interesting for adults. Landscape architect Herb Schaal, a nationally recognized leader in the design of gardens for younger visitors, divided the garden into a series of separate spaces, each with its own identity and focus. The whale terrace, in addition to three spouting, multi-ton leviathans, features swinging benches and a garden of big-leaved plants. Below is the seagull pavilion—one of three structures in this garden with a living roof. It is used as an informal picnic area as well as a meeting place for classes and small parties. The pavilion is adjacent to the maze lawn, an intricate set of spiraling paving stones set into turf that is bordered on three sides by dense plantings and on the fourth by natural ledge. The learning garden—a distinct area featuring edible plants—was originally intended to be a separate project, but was ultimately merged into part of the Children's Garden. Complete with a small greenhouse and story barn, this section provides produce

OPPOSITE Among the many surprises in the Bibby and Harold Alfond Children's Garden are talk tubes that allow a young visitor to speak into one end while friends listen to her voice coming out the mouth of a carved stone dragon nearby.

for the Kitchen Garden Café as well as for a small food-share program and the local food pantry.

The learning garden is set off by a white picket fence, which also encloses a small cottage garden surrounding a children's-scale play cottage with a prairie-sod roof. From the windows of the structure, you can get glimpses of the colorful rainbow terraces that line a descending path leading visitors to the blueberry islands and pond. Nearby, a fanciful tree house overlooks a "bear cave" and a re-created Wabanaki encampment in the woods fifteen feet below.

Safety is of special importance in the Children's Garden. There is only one entrance and exit and the whole two-acre area is enclosed by fencing, walls, or dense vegetation. When the garden is open, specially trained volunteers along with staff are present to answer questions and scout for problems. Other volunteers staff the library, offer drop-in programs, help with summer camps, and assist the horticulture staff to care for the 20,000 trees, shrubs, and flowers in the garden.

ABOVE Dressed in full fairy regalia for the annual Maine Fairy House Festival in August, four sprites survey the watery world just below.
OPPOSITE Plants of unusual shapes, sizes, and colors dot this magical garden. Here blue wild bugloss (*Anchusa azurea*) frames a view across the Lavender Gambol through a grove of animated weeping spruces and false cypress.

ABOVE *Canna* 'Tropicana' makes a colorful statement just outside the main entrance to the Alfond Children's Garden, attracting youngsters much as the butterfly meadow inside lures its fluttering minions. At right an American lady butterfly pauses on a Mexican sunflower in a dazzling gesture of international cooperation. **OPPOSITE** Touches of whimsey are a hallmark of this garden, which was designed by nationally acclaimed landscape architect Herb Schaal of Colorado. For the entrance to the vegetable garden, for instance, he created an archway out of real garden tools sprouting from oversized watering cans ringed by trowels.

ABOVE Even a picket fence in the Alfond Children's Garden provokes a smile. Designed to entertain and engage children of all ages, this two-acre garden became an instant favorite with both families and school groups from throughout Maine and beyond. At right, this straw-stuffed character bears a striking resemblance to the hero of the children's classic *Down to the Sea with Mr. McGee* and was made by students from Southport Central School for the fall Scarecrow Festival. **OPPOSITE** In the treehouse, boys and girls challenge their fear of heights on a rope walk fifteen feet above the ground (though it seems much higher when you are on it!).

Living roofs thrive atop three structures in the Alfond Children's Garden, including the play cottage. Its prairie dropseed roof is in full splendor in July. OPPOSITE Beguiling and unusual blossoms open throughout the growing season here. This colorful milkweed (*Asclepias speciosa* 'Davis') is a favorite of monarch butterfly caterpillars as well as kids.

Another living roof grows on the Seagull Pavilion. Before it lies the inviting maze lawn, which was inspired by an English design. Entering near the pavilion, visitors—young and old alike—must either turn left or go straight as they attempt to reach the middle of the maze.

ABOVE Old-fashioned hand pumps are fascinating to kids used to faucets and spigots. A set of them in the Alfond Children's Garden beckons youngsters to fill waiting watering cans and buckets. Nearby plants are always very well-watered! Strategically placed benches allow visitors—parents, grandparents, elves—to pause for a minute throughout the garden. **OPPOSITE** With an expression somewhere between anger and laughter, these rusty foxgloves (*Digitalis ferruginea*) are but one of the many intriguing plants chosen to delight visitors here.

Rose & Perennial Garden

T

TRADITIONAL EUROPEAN BOTANICAL GARDENS OFTEN INCLUDED A FORMAL ROSE GARDEN arranged in a geometrical pattern of beds containing various types and colors of roses. Designers at Coastal Maine Botanical Gardens wanted to draw from this tradition, but do it with an informality fitting the site and overall garden plan. The focal point of the Rose & Perennial Garden is a large post-and-beam arbor made from Douglas fir. Climbing roses, native wisteria, clematis, ornamental grapes, and honeysuckle are slowly but surely draping the structure in foliage and flowers. Not surprisingly, it is a popular spot for wedding ceremonies, and word has it that more than one marriage proposal has occurred here, too.

As a group, roses prefer cool, sunny weather and fertile soils. They are prone to several leaf diseases that mar their appearance in all but perfect conditions and for this reason they have fallen out of favor throughout much of the U.S. where hot, humid summers encourage diseases and curb vigor. The cooling maritime influence along coastal Maine helps roses fare better here than farther south and west. However, what has really made a rose garden possible here is a quiet revolution in rose breeding that has produced a new generation of vigorous, disease-resistant shrub roses that have breathed new life into this most cherished of garden plants. Most of the varieties are of this improved type. They are winter-hardy, often bloom nearly nonstop through the season, and require no more care than many other flowering shrubs in the collections.

To add more variety to the plantings, perennials, vines, and long-blooming annuals are interspersed among the roses. These have the added benefit of attracting and feeding small flower flies and wasps that prey on aphids, Japanese beetles, and other rose pests. All the roses receive a late winter pruning to remove old canes and to make spring cleanup and mulching a less thorny task.

OPPOSITE Very hardy and wonderfully fragrant, Lillian Gibson roses drape over one corner of the rose arbor. This elegant structure, hand-hewn by Maine craftsmen out of Douglas fir, has become an icon for Coastal Maine Botanical Gardens.

ABOVE Meandering paths within the Rose & Perennial Garden lure walkers of every size. **OPPOSITE** For visiting fairies, the shell-pink blossoms of *Rosa* 'The Fairy' complement their tulle tutus. This polyantha rose blooms in profusion during June and continues on and off until Halloween.

ABOVE The Rose & Perennial Garden comes into peak bloom in June, when delphiniums, astilbes, and other perennials set off the roses splendidly. **OPPOSITE** Exuberant clematis blossoms (*Clematis* 'Multi Blue') weave through the climbing roses on the arbor.

ABOVE Among the myriad kinds of roses that welcome brides and grooms is *Rosa* 'Earthsong,' a long-blooming grandiflora variety. **OPPOSITE** It's hardly a surprise that the rose arbor has become a very popular site for wedding ceremonies all summer long. What setting could be more romantic?

Lerner Garden
of the
Five Senses

T

THE LERNER GARDEN OF THE FIVE SENSES OPENED IN JUNE 2009 AFTER MANY YEARS IN the planning and a generous gift from media executive Daniel Lerner and his wife Lyn of Maine, Pennsylvania, and Florida. Designed by noted landscape architect Herb Schaal, of Colorado, and less than an acre in size, it has meandering paths and a changing elevation that make it seem much larger. The paths circle around through five distinct regions designed to emphasize each of the senses, descending slowly to a weir separating two ponds before rising again to the exit. The garden has been carefully designed to be horticulturally interesting and fun for all visitors no matter what their level of physical ability.

Visitors pass first through the olfactory "node" after entering the garden through a larch-covered archway. Plants such as lilies, daphnes, lilacs, and hyacinths, all known for their fragrant flowers, highlight this most sensory of the five senses, as do aromatic herbs such as lavender, thyme, and mint. Next is the taste node, featuring edible fruits, vegetables, and flowers that guests are encouraged to sample. Raised planters are designed for ease of access by participants in the Gardens' horticultural therapy program, which is housed in the pavilion that helps define this space.

Farther down the path and at the high point of this garden begins the sight node. Here, masses of brightly colored flowers frame panoramic views of the garden and spaces beyond. As the path descends to the center of the Garden of the Five Senses, visitors come upon a reflexology labyrinth that marks the beginning of the tactile node. In addition to the labyrinth, soft-leaved plants, stonework, and the cascade of water over the weir beckon to be touched.

Sound is the most difficult sense to celebrate with plants, but the final node features a more subdued color palette and a large sitting area to encourage guests to pause and listen. Gray tree frogs flocked to the ponds even as they were still

OPPOSITE With different sections or 'nodes' appealing to each of our five senses, this garden features imposing vertical planters in the taste node that have proved tempting to all visitors. A couple of years ago they were planted with an array of mints—and the pineapple mint was a favorite of these judges.

being built, and their shrill birdlike trills combined with the buzz of katydids and croak of green frogs add an unplanned musical ambiance. The primary attraction here is a pair of sound stones. These chiseled pillars of granite have cylindrical holes carved into them, and if you place your face in one and hum, the sound reverberates so loudly it can be heard from the nearby event lawn.

   Though not noticeable to many, there are several features in this garden designed to facilitate its use by physically challenged guests. This was the first garden to feature brick paving, for instance. Changes in paving surface and pattern help guide visually impaired visitors while providing a smooth, hard surface and gentle slope for wheeled mobility aids. The fountain in the upper pond provides a constant sound to help orient those who cannot see, while ample opportunities for tactile as well as visual stimulation delight those who cannot hear. The raised beds in the horticultural therapy area have cutaways underneath so that participants in wheelchairs can slide in close in much the same way as one sits at a desk. These "tabletop" beds are excellent for fast crops of greens and herbs that do not need much soil.

ABOVE Spikes of golden leopard plant (*Ligularia* 'Little Rocket') and white daylily (*Hemerocallis* 'Joan Senior') bloom along the path leading from the touch to the sound nodes.
OPPOSITE Rich blue *Lobelia* 'Lucia Dark Blue' contrasts with chartreuse *Sedum rupestre* 'Lemon Coral' in two vertical planters.

ABOVE LEFT Brightly colored flowers and 'sentinel' stones near the entrance to the Lerner Garden of the Five Senses make it more visible to visually impaired guests. **ABOVE RIGHT** A tall, granite sound stone, one of two at the center of the hearing node, has cylindrical holes carved into it that allow the tones from visitors humming into it to reverberate across the garden. **OPPOSITE** *Polygonatum kingianum*, an unusual species of Solomon's seal with brightly colored flowers, flourishes near the beginning of the sight node.

A Pond from Scratch

The ponds in the Lerner Garden of the Five Senses—along with all the other water features at the Gardens—are manmade. Most were constructed using a flexible rubber liner that was cut to size and spread inside an excavated depression. For added strength, the ponds in the Garden of the Five Senses were then sprayed with a coating of concrete. Two large pumps in an underground vault near the center of the garden pump hundreds of gallons a minute up to the rill under the tree bridge and through the fountain. The water flows over the weir and under the path into the lower pond whence it is pumped back up to the top. Aeration from the fountain and rapid water movement help prevent stagnation while adding greatly to the audial experience. Though a few dozen golden shiners were transferred from the forest pond, all the other pond life save the water lilies found its way to the water very quickly on its own. Within a week of construction, frogs had already laid eggs in the pools and dragonflies could be seen flitting above the surface in courtship dances.

OPPOSITE Three bold but complementary varieties of daylily attract the eye in midsummer in the Lerner Garden of the Five Senses. **ABOVE LEFT** In the touch node is a circular reflexology labyrinth. Its rounded stones become smaller as one approaches the center, and walking on them is best accomplished barefoot. **ABOVE RIGHT** The delicate blooms of meadow rue (*Thalictrum grandiflorum*) almost demand close study.

ABOVE Although most familiar in hanging baskets, fuchsias work well here in the garden beds. The red fuchsia 'Gartenmeister Bonstedt' is combined with the maroon rhubarb 'Ace of Hearts.'
OPPOSITE Creeping phlox (*Phlox stolonifera* 'Sherwood Purple') rings the upper pond with amethyst during the month of May.

Paving stones of different widths guide those using white canes, and the hard surface is a help for wheelchair-bound visitors. The entire entrance arch will someday be covered with a soft curtain of weeping larch (*Larix decidua* 'Pendula'), a dramatic spectacle for the sighted and a tactile signal marking the entryway for the visually impaired.

Slater
Forest Pond

T

THE AREA THAT WOULD BECOME THE SLATER FOREST POND, LOCATED JUST OFF THE GREAT Lawn, was a naturally low spot that proved to be perfect for a small pond. Though some of the native vegetation was preserved during construction in 2006, the pond itself was excavated and lined, then replanted with appropriate shrubs, trees, and pond plants. It is amazing to compare pictures from its earliest years when the plantings looked sparse to what the pond looks like today with vegetation so thick the water itself is almost hidden from view until you are almost at its edge. The pond quickly filled with frogs and aquatic insects, and the large stepping stones set into the water were such an instant favorite with children that similar ones were incorporated into the Alfond Children's Garden, too. More than one parent has had to pull a laughing but dripping child from these stones after a pond-side hunt for critters. Some wonder if small ponds such as this are breeding grounds for mosquitos. Fortunately, minnows, dragonfly nymphs, and other predators keep the mosquito larvae at bay. Mosquitos prefer less dangerous places like swampy pools and puddles.

Plants that grow in shallow water and along the shore are called emergent or semi-aquatic because though their roots are submerged, their tops rise above the surface. This group includes many sedges, reeds, and some flowers, including pickerelweed and water arum that help to hold the bank and reduce erosion while giving the pond edge a more natural look. Planting emergent species can be challenging as they easily float away until their roots take hold in the mud. At the Gardens, they are planted in the mud at water's edge and held down with stones placed atop their roots until roots establish. The most obvious truly aquatic plants in this pond are the beautiful water lilies whose sweetly scented flowers appear continuously throughout the summer. These water lilies are all forms of our native species so they are completely winter hardy.

OPPOSITE The elegant, pure white spathe of the wild calla lily (*Calla palustris*) seems a bit incongruous sprouting from pond-side mud. This native arum is related to the tropical calla lilies favored by floral designers.

True harbingers of spring, yellow marsh marigolds (*Caltha palustris*) bloom prolifically around the Slater Forest Pond in April.

OPPOSITE The semi-aquatic giant bullrush *(Schoenoplectus tabernaemontani* 'Albescens') was originally planted on the bank of the rill but has now migrated into the shallow water.

ABOVE Just after completion of the Slater Forest Pond, it was possible to view across to the Rose Garden and Great Lawn. That is no longer the case, as the plantings matured quickly and now screen the pond almost completely. **OPPOSITE** Later in the season *Nymphaea* 'Indiana' is one of the beautifully colored hardy water lilies that blossom here.

ABOVE New artworks appear in the Gardens each year. Maine artist Eric Hopkins installed his glass sculpture *Helios* in the Slater Forest Pond for the 2007 summer sculpture show. **OPPOSITE** In the foreground are white turtlehead (*Chelone glabra*) and blue lobelia (*Lobelia siphilitica*), two of the wetland wildflowers planted along the watercourse connected to the pond.

Burpee
Kitchen
Garden

T

THE CONCEPT OF A KITCHEN GARDEN IS PROBABLY AS OLD AS AGRICULTURE ITSELF. Planting herbs, vegetables, fruits, and even medicinal plants within easy reach of the kitchen can be as simple as scattering a few seeds in the dooryard or cultivating a window box or two. Thanks to a gift from the Burpee Foundation, the corporate giving foundation of the famous W. Atlee Burpee Seed Company, this garden was begun as part of the Visitor Center construction in 2006. To meet the demands of our café and provide it with signature herbs, edible flowers, fruits, and vegetables, it was located where the chefs could access it easily. You will notice that unlike any other area at the Gardens, it is based on a symmetrical, rectilinear design. Every year horticulture staff and volunteers plant the beds with a selection of low, edible plants requested by the café chef and arrange them in the fashion of a parterre. In 2012 the wall that surrounds the garden was extended to create a more intimate atmosphere. At the same time some beds were expanded and café tables were added to invite diners not only to taste the fruits of this garden, but to enjoy their food in it as well.

After the first frosts of autumn, beds are cleaned up and 1,500 tulip bulbs are planted to provide color in late April and May. The tulips finish just in time for spring planting. Once they are removed, fresh compost is dug in and vegetables, herbs, and edible flowers are set out in esoteric patterns. The most successful designs employ compact varieties with colored or very textural foliage to create contrast. Favorites include colored Swiss chard, red leaf lettuce, nasturtiums, lemon gem marigolds, tricolor sage, miniature basil, dwarf cabbages, creeping rosemary, and golden-leaved thyme.

Some visitors ask why there are not more rectilinear, symmetrical gardens elsewhere at the Gardens. This type of design is most effective on flat sites, but it becomes very challenging when attempted on the sort of hilly, rocky land that underlies Coastal Maine Botanical Gardens.

OPPOSITE
As colorful as it is tasty, 'Bright Lights' Swiss chard is a favorite for Kitchen Garden planting designs.

ABOVE Customers of the Kitchen Garden Café can relax with a beverage or meal on the terrace surrounded by the large white inflorescences of 'Annabelle' hydrangea. Many of the ingredients of the fare served are grown right here. **OPPOSITE** Among the edibles cultivated in the Kitchen Garden is a variety of dwarf eggplant. The flowers of the plant are quite pretty, which is a good thing as the fruits are tricky to produce in Maine's cool climate.

ABOVE LEFT Regal lilies (*Lilium regale*) and 'Rozanne' geraniums are among the purely ornamental plants that grow at the margins of the kitchen terrace. **ABOVE RIGHT** Other ornamentals include pale orange angel's trumpet (*Brugmansia sp.*) and bronze New Zealand sedge (*Carex flagellifera* 'Toffee Twist'). **OPPOSITE** Delicious purple raspberries (*Rubus idaeus* 'Royalty'), intriguingly complex to look at up close, grow within easy reach of kitchen staff.

Great Lawn

T

THE CONCEPT OF A "GREAT LAWN" HARKENS BACK TO NINETEENTH-CENTURY LANDSCAPE parks modeled after pastoral landscapes. Quite simply, a great lawn is a large area of turf bordered by forest and plantings. Besides offering the obvious advantage of a large open space near the Visitor Center for events and gatherings, the Great Lawn here was designed to create a sense of scale and a feeling of openness in marked contrast to the densely wooded entrance drive. Since this grass oval lies at the heart of the central gardens, unobstructed views help first-time visitors orient themselves as they begin their visit.

One of the most distinctive features of the Great Lawn is Whale Rock, a massive formation of Bucksport schist that rises out of the grass at the southern edge of the lawn and, yes, suggests the shape of a whale's back. Bucksport schist along with granite are the primary bedrock types underlying the Gardens. The schist originated as sediments deep in the ocean, and the rock has a distinctive layered appearance. Fortunately, the Gardens' planners decided not to blast this rock to create a lawn that was completely level. Children love to play "king of the mountain" here, and adults simply like to climb up and see just a little farther than they can from the lawn below.

The plantings that surround the lawn feature broad sweeps of perennials and grasses suggesting a stylized meadow to complement the adjoining turf. One notable departure from this design is the oval Founders Grove, located just beyond the Visitor Center steps. This subdued planting of seven narrow pin oaks, blueberries, and grasses was commissioned to quietly honor the founders of the Gardens for their foresight and determination. Many visitors are hesitant to tread on the grass of the Great Lawn, but all should feel free to walk, play, and picnic on this soft expanse of green in the heart of the Gardens.

ABOVE The Great Lawn is the site of the maypole dance, performed here by students from the Portland School of Ballet, during the annual Maine Fairy House Festival each August at Coastal Maine Botanical Gardens. **OPPOSITE** Vibrant annuals, purple butterfly bushes, and yellow coneflowers blend with grasses in this stylized meadow along the edge of the Great Lawn.

ABOVE LEFT Executive director William Cullina and son Ronan watch the festivities on the Great Lawn. **ABOVE RIGHT** Plantings that abut the Great Lawn offer a contrast of color and texture that helps define the expanse of neatly trimmed turf. This drift of yellow and white 'Rex Ray' tulips includes some of the 14,000 bulbs planted each year for April and May bloom. **OPPOSITE** A dwarf tulip (*Tulipa* 'Little Beauty') not far from the Great Lawn greets early spring visitors.

Organic Lawn Care

Starting in 2009, the lawns at the Gardens have been managed organically—without synthetic pesticides and fertilizers. The Great Lawn has always been especially challenging to maintain as it was installed over the site of the staging area used during the construction of the Visitor Center and surrounding gardens. In 2006, piles of rock and soil taller than the building sat where grass now grows, severely compacting the ground. As a consequence, grass roots have difficulty penetrating deeper than a few inches. To help alleviate soil compaction, the horticulture staff uses what is called a plug-aerator to drill small holes through the thatch into which they rake fresh compost. They are also seeding more rugged fescue grasses into the beautiful but fussy bluegrass. After just three years, this treatment is having a noticeably positive effect on turf health.

Shoreland Trail

F FROM 1995 WHEN THE PROPERTY FOR THE COASTAL MAINE BOTANICAL GARDENS WAS purchased, until 2001 when work on what would become the Giles Rhododendron Garden began in earnest, garden volunteers focused primarily on developing a trail system along the waterfront and through nearby woods and wetlands. Later christened the Shoreland Trail, this network of more than three miles of footpaths takes visitors though some of the Gardens' most beautiful forests and ledges and along nearly the entire length of its mile-long waterfront. Though augmented with some native plantings early on, for the most part this trail system showcases trees, shrubs, wildflowers, ferns, and mosses indigenous to the property. As the ornamental gardens near the Visitor Center developed, this waterfront zone has been kept intentionally wild and quintessentially Maine in quiet counterpoint to the color and drama of the central gardens.

During the initial trail construction, workers discovered a two-acre area with an abundance of wild pink lady's slippers *(Cypripedium acaule)*. These showy orchids grew in an area that had been partially cleared by land developers to open up water views for prospective homebuyers. Increased light had encouraged the lady's slippers, and by 2000 they were blooming by the hundreds. Beginning in 1998, Dr. Joanne Sharpe, a botanist who specializes in plant population biology, recruited a cadre of volunteers to begin a detailed study of the orchids, counting flowers, seedlings, and the number of plants in three distinct colonies — a study that continues to this day. The most prolific of these colonies grows in what is now the Reiser Lady's-slipper Glen, and visitors flock to it each spring to see these enchanting, mysterious plants. Not surprisingly, when the Gardens were fenced in 2007 to exclude voracious deer, the number of blooming plants began to skyrocket within the 60-acre fenced area.

OPPOSITE In summer, prevailing winds bring fog in from the ocean on many afternoons, fostering the conifer forest and indigenous plant life along the Gardens' mile-long shoreline.

In 2008 the Shoreland Trail was extended south through the Jeffords Preserve, a 120-acre property that had been donated to the Gardens three years earlier by Sally Jeffords, of Southport Island, Maine, president of the Pine Tree Conservation Society (a local land stewardship organization). This trail extension provided an opportunity to experiment with a new type of path material called Superhumus that is a byproduct of the timber industry. The technique succeeded in greatly decreasing root damage to trees along what is now known as the Huckleberry Cove Trail and is currently being adopted for trail construction throughout the shoreland zone. Named the Huckleberry Cove Trail because it terminates at a small cove bordered by black huckleberries, the path takes visitors through dense boreal forest and near immense granite outcrops dripping with moss, lichens, and the diminutive polypody fern. Near Huckleberry Cove, trailheads for several more rustic hiking trails take intrepid explorers deeper into the mossy woods.

ABOVE On an autumn afternoon Huckleberry Cove offers a peaceful respite.
OPPOSITE One of the first structures built at the Gardens was this wooden bridge over a small stream near the shore. Beyond lies a test garden for ferns, a continuing collaboration between the Hardy Fern Foundation in Washington State and Coastal Maine Botanical Gardens.

ABOVE LEFT & RIGHT Red chanterelles and orange amanitas are but two of many mushroom species that call these woods home. October is the best month to look for the fleeting fungi. **OPPOSITE** Bloodroot (*Sanguinaria canadensis*) is a cherished Maine wildflower that was planted by volunteers along part of the Shoreland Trail in the earliest days of the Gardens. It has naturalized along the path leading to the bridge.

Fairy Houses

Early on, staffers at the Gardens were surprised to discover fanciful little structures known locally as fairy houses dotting the Shoreland Trail with some regularity. Crafted from twigs, bark, cones, and leaves, these rustic dwellings were left for whatever elfin denizens of the Maine woods might need cover. The tradition, it is widely held, originated in the woods on Monhegan Island, located just twelve miles off the coast from Boothbay Harbor. While some dispute that, the popularity of building these houses has spread throughout Maine, and the Shoreland Trail at the Gardens was soon overwhelmed by fairy house "sprawl." To contain the houses and keep builders from plundering the Gardens for construction materials, a "village" of fairy houses was established just off the trail near the water. Staff now stock the village with building materials and let young visitors do the rest. The popularity of the fairy houses spurred the annual Fairy House Festival the first weekend in August, as well as an additional village in the backwoods areas of the Alfond Children's Garden.

Giles Rhododendron Garden

T

THE GILES RHODODENDRON AND PERENNIAL GARDEN NESTLES INTO A HILLSIDE ON THE northeastern edge of Coastal Maine Botanical Gardens about a third of a mile from the central gardens that surround the main buildings. The location is comfortably removed from the hubbub, allowing visitors a quiet amble through its winding paths up a hillside featuring more than a thousand rhododendrons and related shrubs as well as a tremendous spring bulb display. This has not always been the case. The pond that now serves as a focal point for the garden was created when the developer who originally owned the property dug gravel to create an entrance road, which began at the gate now closed off at the eastern end of the garden. Thus, until the entrance road was re-routed in 2006, the Rhododendron Garden was literally the front entrance of the Gardens.

The late Ernie Egan, one of the founders of the Gardens and a former president of the American Rhododendron Society, first introduced the idea of a garden featuring rhododendrons and companion plants. A professional horticulturist with a family home in Boothbay, Egan knew from personal experience that the cool, damp climate and thin soils of the Boothbay Peninsula were well-suited for rhododendron culture. He helped the Gardens select the original 100 plants that became the nucleus for a collection that now comprises 250 species and varieties and nearly 2,000 individual plants. Though most of the larger shrubs are considered "ironclads" (varieties with notable winter hardiness), many other species and cultivars yet untested in Maine are planted here as well.

The original plants were sited on the slope to the west of the pond and plantings have been gradually expanding outward in all directions. This expansion has not always been easy. When the grounds crew began working on the hillside above the pond, they soon hit immovable rock—part of the steep ledge that underlies the

OPPOSITE
Rhododendron 'Zoe Graves' was among the many mature rhododendrons donated by avid hybridizer Ernie Egan, who served as first board president of Coastal Maine Botanical Gardens in 1992.

hillside. Rather than scrap the idea of building this garden on this spot, however, they created terraces bordered by low stone walls to retain the soil and plantings. Broad stone steps lead to and from one side of the pond, where a weighty stone bench allows visitors to admire the view and watch the pond, spotting a frog here, a frog there, and then, once they have the knack of finding them, frogs just about everywhere.

The Giles Rhododendron Garden is one of the first to come into bloom in early spring. Hellebores and a plethora of spring bulbs carpet the ground from late March until May, when the flowering shrubs begin to come into their glory. Hostas, ferns, epimediums, and many other shade plants provide textural interest through the summer months. In 2007, a dramatic waterfall designed by landscape architect Bruce John Riddell, then of Bar Harbor and now headquartered in Boothbay Harbor, was added as a tribute to long-time board members and fundraising leaders John and Sarah Giles, and it quickly became one of the most popular spots on the entire property.

ABOVE Early morning is a magical time in the Gardens throughout the year. Here light reflects off the pond in October. **OPPOSITE** Among the nearly 2,000 specimens in the Giles Rhododendron Garden is *Rhododendron pseudochrysanthum*, an uncommon dwarf species noted for the lovely fuzz or indumentum that coats emerging leaves.

OPPOSITE In late May and early June, this garden is resplendent with many of the larger rhododendrons in full flower. **ABOVE LEFT AND RIGHT** Among other plants growing here are thick-stemmed wood fern (*Dryopteris crassirhizoma*), which blends with Spanish bluebells (*Hyacinthoides hispanica* 'Excelsior') along the steps, and vivid blue Siberian bugloss (*Brunnera macrophylla* 'Silver Wings').

Diminutive blooms of a small barrenwort (*Epimedium diphyllum* 'Nanum') delight observant visitors in May. OPPOSITE Wine red flowers of the hellebore 'Winter Dreams Cassis Red' appear in March on the sunny, southeast-facing hillside.

ABOVE New spring foliage in the woods is the perfect foil for the exuberant early rhododendron blooms. Trails and rock work wind and climb throughout the terrain here. **OPPOSITE** A distant relative of rhododendrons, *Menziesia ciliicalyx* 'Plum Drops' thrives under the same growing conditions in which they prosper.

Cleaver
Event Lawn
& Garden

ONE OF THE RESPONSIBILITIES OF A BOTANICAL GARDEN IS TO BUILD RESEARCH collections of certain plants. Thanks to the guidance and enthusiasm of some of our early volunteers, the first we established was our collection of kousa dogwood (*Benthamidia japonica*). This lovely small tree—a relative of our native flowering dogwood—blooms from June into mid-July and the large, pure white flowers have an undeniably matrimonial aspect. Weddings are regularly held here in the summer months, so it seemed natural to marry the first plant collection with a ceremonial space large enough to accommodate several hundred guests. With a gift from the Cleaver family of Southport Island, construction on the Cleaver Event Lawn began in 2008. From a design perspective, it was a challenging spot in that the garden beds slope away from the turf area. So, while the view from the grass is lovely, the vista looking up at the masses of perennials and flowering shrubs is even better from the Lerner Garden of the Five Senses located below. In keeping with the celebratory theme of this garden, the planting design relies heavily on white, as well as pastel pink, yellow, and blue-flowered species. One of the focal points of this garden is the grove of golden-leaved dawn redwood (*Metasequoia glyptostroboides* 'Ogon'). Now restricted in the wild to just a few places in China, this relict species of the Cretaceous period was once widespread in what is now North America. The golden-leaved form is an unusual variant that is especially vibrant on a cloudy or foggy day.

Adjacent to the Cleaver Event Lawn is a smaller oval of turf commonly referred to as the ceremonial lawn. A fieldstone terrace bordering moss-covered outcrops here is used for smaller formal gatherings. The woodland area just to the north of the lawn has been carefully edited to showcase a dozen species of native mosses along with companion plants.

OPPOSITE Like many plants in the Gardens, native blue flag irises (*Iris versicolor*) appeared here on their own. That was not the case, however, with the weeping copper beeches standing like sentinels behind them.

ABOVE The Cleaver Event Lawn is large enough to accommodate tents for up to 200. **OPPOSITE** A sizable collection of pagoda dogwoods (*Benthamidia japonica*), including this lovely cultivar 'Blue Shadow,' rings the lawn and the adjacent Woodland Garden. Longtime volunteer and local dogwood enthusiast Merlin Smith first suggested the notion of a dogwood collection during the Gardens' 1998 planning charrette. The pure white to pink flowers of these small trees provide a perfect background for the functions held here.

By early September, perennials have grown over the edges of many paths on the hill below the lawn. Golden dawn redwoods, performing very well in Maine, are visible in the background.

Regal lilies and ostrich feather astilbe (*Astilbe thunbergii* 'Straussenfeder') typify the soft color palette chosen for this festive location. OPPOSITE Come fall, hardy mums (*Chrysanthemum* 'Cambodian Queen') echo the pink of the June-flowering astilbes while willowleaf bluestar (*Amsonia hubrichtii*) turns shades of mango and lemon.

Haney
Hillside
Garden

S

SOME OF THE FIRST THINGS VISITORS APPRECIATE ABOUT COASTAL MAINE BOTANICAL Gardens are the massive ledges and outcrops that dominate the property. The land lies atop an old fault line formed when one section of the earth's crust slammed into another at gradual but relentless geological speed. The pressure of this slow-motion collision fractured and uplifted the rock, creating steep cliffs that run north to south and slope generally to the west. Over time these cliffs eroded and softened, but they still have enough presence to impart dramatic topography and elevation changes. The central gardens are built on a plateau that sits 100 feet above the sea just to the east of this fault. Originally, the plan was to construct the Visitor Center at the edge of the precipice to offer views out over the Sheepscot River, though that plan proved impractical and the building site was moved to its present location. To allow access to the water below, a descending path connecting a series of terraces was planned. The dramatic fractured ledge provided a strong framework for gardens that would develop out of the dense boreal forest that flanked the slope.

With a generous gift from board members and retired executives from the fields of journalism and finance Dan and Susan Haney, construction on the Haney Hillside Garden began in 2005. The sheer challenge of constructing a garden on a steep, rocky hillside made it the Gardens' most logistically difficult project completed to date. The design by Bruce John Riddell features three terraces, or landings, linking 1,000 feet of switchback paths set between the major outcrops of ledge. The first, the water terrace, features a small waterfall trickling through clefts into a granite basin. Next is the moss terrace, a paved oval nestled into the rocky slope that surrounds a bed of haircap moss and ferns. The final terrace showcases a large glass orb, by New York sculptor Henry Richardson, that seems to glow as if lit

OPPOSITE Swaths of Maine blueberries (*Vaccinium angustifolium*) thrive in the thin soils over the ledge found on this part of the garden.

within no matter what the weather. Together, the three landings loosely symbolize the three primal elements of water, earth, and fire.

This garden opened in 2006, but as luck would have it, the infamous Patriot's Day storm of April 2007 wreaked havoc on the exposed hillside. Heavy wet snow and saturated ground coupled with high winds brought down dozens of mature evergreens, turning what was a lovely woodland path into a scene of twisted destruction. To remedy this, the garden was completely renovated in 2010 and 2011. Paths were reworked, stone walls erected, and 6,000 native plants installed to complement the magnificent natural ledges and original terraces. More clearly than anywhere else on the property, the overall design intent of Coastal Maine Botanical Gardens is evident in the Haney Hillside Garden: to cluster intensive gardens around the central campus and leave the shoreland areas primarily natural. The uppermost sections of the hillside are the most intensively planted while the lower areas near the water rely primarily on careful editing of the natural vegetation for effect.

ABOVE The moss landing in the Haney Hillside Garden features intricate Maine stone paving designed by Bruce John Riddell, one of the earliest of the landscape architects employed by the Gardens.
OPPOSITE A newer feature is this bog pool. The acidic soils surrounding it stay very wet, supporting such bog natives as cranberries and leatherleaf.

ABOVE Brilliant red mountain laurel (*Kalmia latifolia* 'Keepsake') is perfectly at home on the steep, rocky terrain. Plantings also include drifts of New York aster (*Symphyotrichum novi-belgii*), some 200 of which were added in 2011. **OPPOSITE** A favorite of many visitors to this garden is the hillside of weeping trees. Pictured is a weeping larch, the same type planted at the entrance to the Lerner Garden of the Five Senses.

ABOVE Near the bottom of the Haney Hillside Garden, cultivated plantings transition to natural woodland as the path descends to the waterfront just beyond. **OPPOSITE** Magnolia 'Yellow Lantern' is a striking hybrid of the wild cucumber tree. It can be found about midway down the path below the weeping trees.

Vayo Meditation Garden

B

BOUNDARIES BETWEEN LAND AND WATER—BE THEY BEACH, HEADLAND, OR MARSH—HAVE an undeniably calming effect on the psyche. Out of respect for this, and to provide a quiet retreat for those seeking the tranquility of the shore, a meditative garden was conceived as part of the early planning in 1998. Originally sited just yards from the shoreline, this garden was to be a quiet respite from all the color and bustle of the central gardens, featuring rock, mosses, ferns, and other ground covers.

In the nineteenth century, coastal Maine was home to numerous granite quarries. The durable stone was cut and blasted from deposits near the ocean and sailed to burgeoning cities along the Atlantic seaboard hungry for the raw material needed to construct great buildings. Statehouses, banks, and office buildings from Boston to Chicago were built with Maine granite—even the Washington Monument contains some of it. As the age of stone yielded to the age of steel and concrete, these quarries were mostly abandoned. When conceiving of the meditation garden, landscape architect Bruce John Riddell had the notion to bring in large blocks from a representative number of these old quarries in homage to this forgotten age. After a hundred years lying abandoned in quarries stretching from the midcoast to the shore and islands Down East, these old blocks are covered in lichens and moss that obscure the pinks, grays, whites, and blacks of the individual stones.

After a gift from the Vayo family, of nearby Sawyer Island, construction on the garden began in 2005. All the stone had to be hauled down the hillside piece by piece, a task made even more challenging by record rainfall during that summer and fall. To complete the garden, a large central basin meticulously carved by Plymouth, Maine, sculptor David Holmes was placed to symbolically unify stone, water, and sky. The basin itself is carved from a soapstone-like rock called Ellsworth schist. This particular boulder was found in a blueberry field near Mount Desert Island.

OPPOSITE A simple stone bench just above the waterline captures the essence of this understated and contemplative garden. Nearby a trail leads walkers to Huckleberry Cove in the distance.

ABOVE Large blocks of granite, shown here in an early view of the Vayo Meditation Garden, are each from a different historic Maine quarry. At one time the state supplied granite for important buildings throughout the eastern half of the nation. In the foreground sits the monumental stone basin carved from a single boulder of Ellsworth schist by Maine sculptor David Holmes.
OPPOSITE Patterned like a spiral of DNA, this path leads through ferns and moss to a stone bench overlooking the garden.

ABOVE The scarlet plumleaf azalea (*Rhododendron prunifolium*) is unusual in that it flowers in August. Blue wood anemone (*Anemone nemorosa* 'Ginny') and other ground covers creep around the stones and through the woods here. **OPPOSITE** The soft texture and color of various ferns contrast with the visual weight of the massive granite blocks. Ferns relish the damp atmosphere along the Maine shore.

Water View

The shore below the Vayo Meditation Garden is a small section of the property's extensive saltwater coastline. What you see when you look out from the garden is called the Back River, a section of the larger Sheepscot River that flows around an island chain running south from Wiscasset. The two islands directly across from the garden are Hodgdon Island to the north and Sawyer Island to the south. The tides in this part of Maine run 8 to 10 feet, so while at low tide the river is quite shallow, at high tide it is 15 to 20 feet deep. A new, higher bridge just to the north of this site has made this section of the river more accessible to small boats. Occasionally, you might even see a seaweed-harvesting boat vacuuming up rockweed near the shore to be sold and processed to extract carrageenan, a gelatinous material used as an additive in a variety of food products.

VAYO MEDITATION GARDEN 171

Woodland
Garden

S

SURROUNDING THE CEREMONIAL LAWN AND JUST WEST OF THE CLEAVER EVENT LAWN IS the beginning of the Woodland Garden. Though small as of this writing, plans are to expand this garden substantially in the coming years.

Gardening under trees has its share of challenges. These forest giants capture most of the available sunlight, nutrients, and water, leaving little for the shrubs, flowers, ferns, and mosses growing in their shade. To even the playing field, one of the first tasks when installing a woodland garden is to remove some of the trees. Individuals that have disease or structural problems and smaller ones that are weak or crowded are removed first. The remaining trees are limbed up with pole saws or by trained climbers using ropes. The goal is to remove the lowest twenty to thirty feet of branches, which further opens the canopy and gives the space a loftier, vaulted feeling. Light levels on the forest floor double, while root competition for water and nutrients is cut in half. Deciduous trees such as oaks, maples, and ashes have some advantages over evergreens such as pines and spruce as more light gets to the forest floor in early spring before they leaf out. However, at the Gardens the aim is to preserve a diversity of tree species if possible.

Because most forest soils in coastal Maine are thin, often the soil needs to be amended and improved to cultivate all but the most rugged native understory plants. The easiest way to accomplish this is to bring in topsoil amended with compost. As much as twelve inches of soil can be spread atop tree roots without causing harm as long as the soil is kept at least three feet away from trunks. Ideally, soil augmentation should be completed in the fall when the ground is drier and the beds left to settle over the winter before being planted in the spring.

OPPOSITE Gardening beneath trees can be a challenge, but some plants flourish in these shady conditions. Chinese fairy wings (*Disporum cantonense*), for example, happily bloom in the shade of a large white pine.

ABOVE A large moosewood (*Acer pensylvanicum*) turns soft yellow as the nights cool in autumn. A lovely native tree, it has very ornamental green and white bark that is especially noticeable during the winter months. This maple grows well in the understory beneath taller trees. **OPPOSITE** Witch hazel (*Hamamelis x intermedia* 'Magic Fire') flowers through the February snow. The thin petals roll up on cold days and unroll when the temperature rises.

Exotic blooms of the pink jack-in-the-pulpit (*Arisaema candidissimum*) are thrilling to come upon in the Woodland Garden during the late spring. OPPOSITE This shelter was installed for an art show here one summer and promptly disassembled afterward, even though it looked as though it had always been there. One of the many charms of Coastal Maine Botanical Gardens is its ever-changing appearance.

Bosarge Family
Education Center

W

WITH THE INCREASING POPULARITY OF THE GARDENS' EDUCATION PROGRAMS AND THE organization's growing staff, it became clear as early as 2008 that more office and meeting space was needed. The possibility of building an innovative, super-energy-efficient education center caught the attention of Dr. Ed Bosarge, mathematician, entrepreneur, and longtime champion of green energy. When the Bosarge Family Education Center opened in July 2011, it was billed as the "greenest building in Maine" because of its use of innovative energy-generating and energy-saving systems coupled with sustainable construction materials and design. The designers of the building, Maclay Architects of Waitsfield, Vermont, and Scott Simons Architects of Portland, Maine, incorporated a photovoltaic array that generates 45 kilowatts of electricity (about the same as generated by the engine in a small hybrid car), which is enough to meet all the energy needs of the building. Thick insulated walls and ceilings provide 50 percent more insulation than is standard, and super-efficient heat pumps provide heating and cooling. State-of-the-art high-efficiency lighting reduces electricity use by 60 percent and rainwater recapture contributes to a 75-percent savings in water use compared to a conventional building of similar size. The building received coveted Leadership in Energy and Environmental Design (LEED) platinum status from the U.S. Green Building Council, and the expectation is that after a one-year audit is completed it will be classified as a net-zero building, signifying that it generates at least as much energy as it consumes in a calendar year.

The gardens that surround the Bosarge Family Education Center utilize native plants selected for their adaptability to the various microclimates presented here. Several basins are designed to collect rainwater and allow it to slowly percolate downward into the soil rather than to run off.

OPPOSITE Solar panels on the roof of the Bosarge Family Education Center, along with another array of them nearby, meet virtually all the energy needs of this extraordinary, ecologically sensitive building. Native trees on the surrounding grounds, including showy mountain ash (*Sorbus decora*), were chosen for their adaptability to existing site conditions.

ABOVE Skylights on the north side of the classroom roof let in copious light, but have retractable shades to darken the room if needed. **OPPOSITE** The curious, ball-shaped inflorescences of buttonbush (*Cephalanthus occidentalis*) appear in summer near the south terrace. This adaptable native shrub can grow in standing water, making it a perfect choice for the rainwater basins that surround the Bosarge Family Education Center.

What's Next?

WE HAVE COME SO FAR IN SUCH A SHORT AMOUNT OF TIME, SO IT IS NATURAL TO ask what the future holds for Coastal Maine Botanical Gardens. No one has a crystal ball and predictions are always a tad risky, but looking at all that has been accomplished in the last twenty years and at the continually growing strengths of the organization, the future looks very bright indeed.

We want to build on the Gardens' three core focus areas: horticultural innovation, educational excellence, and thoughtful, applied research. We want to continue to be regarded as a progressive, twenty-first-century botanical garden, embracing technology but not being heartily seduced by it, building on horticultural traditions without being inordinately constrained by them, and most of all celebrating this unique, enigmatic, and truly charismatic place called Maine.

In the next few years, we plan to begin construction of a very different type of garden we are calling the Wild Woodlands of Maine. Sprawling over perhaps twenty-five acres of our property and showcasing seven of our most distinctive and interesting plant communities such as blueberry barrens, bogs, and boreal forests, this will not be a garden in the traditional sense but rather an edited, refined, but still wild slice of coastal Maine. Walking trails and accessible paths will take visitors on an educational journey that will highlight the plants, geology, hydrology, and microclimates that make this place so special.

The metaphor of the journey is an important one to mention, because as I analyze what it is that makes our gardens so popular with visitors, it is this sense of exploration, a layered experience of surprises and discovery around every bend, that seems to play the largest part. We hope to develop more gardens to delight and educate explorers of all ages and physical abilities. Possibilities include a stream garden that uses flowing water as its organizing principle and takes guests over bridges, under waterfalls, and through dense plantings as they follow the meandering course of the water. We also hope to create further connection with our most prominent water feature—the Atlantic Ocean. Whether by dock, boat, or other means, we want to feature both the natural and cultural history of the sea and shore.

Currently lacking from Coastal Maine Botanical Gardens is a true woodland

Acknowledgements

The history of a people's garden is best told through the voices of all the people who have made the dream of Coastal Maine Botanical Gardens a magnificent reality. Although it is impossible to list all the volunteers, staff, and advisors who made this place possible, we especially thank the following friends who took time to be interviewed. We especially thank Susan Simeone, who led the interview process for this book. In addition to providing us a complete and detailed history for this work, we also have pages and pages of quotes, anecdotes, and wonderful stories for our permanent historical archive. We are truly grateful to:

Barbara Alfond	Cynthia Hosmer	Sharmon Provan
Karen Bartholomew	Claire Hunt, Ph.D.	Robbie Roberts
Ed & Marie Bosarge	Pat Jeremiah	Martha Robes
Bob Boyd	Shery Kerr	Susan Russell
Ginger Carr	Dan & Lyn Lerner	Nat & Betsy Saltonstall
John & Sarah Giles	Bruce McElroy	Pat Shubert
Rollie Hale	Mollie & Wells Moore	Larry Townley
Jean Hamilton	Helen Norton	Dick Zieg
Dan & Susan Haney	Donna Phinney	

We want to thank Bob Mitchell, Lynn Karlin, and the other photographers whose work has told our story in pictures even more completely than we can do in words. Special thanks also go to key staff members of the Gardens who provided documentation, text preparation, and fact-checking: Courtney Locke and Jen McKane. We thank the staff at Down East Books. Special thanks go to Dale W. Kuhnert for his editorial guidance and passion for the Gardens. We thank the Coastal Maine Botanical Gardens Board of Directors and the Board of Overseers for their support of this effort to memorialize the history of the Gardens. In particular, we acknowledge the leadership counsel of Board President Susan Reid Russell in bringing this project from concept to completion.

Most of all we want to acknowledge our volunteers, donors, members, and all others who believed in us: THANK YOU! We could not have done it without you.

Bill Cullina
Dorothy E. Freeman, Ph.D.
Barbara Hill Freeman